AFFIRMING YOUR SELF-WORTH

STRATEGIES FOR ACHIEVING EMOTIONAL WELLBEING

DR. JAGADEESH PILLAI

Made with ♥ on the Notion Press Platform
www.notionpress.com

|| Dedicated to all wisdom seekers around the world ||

ꕥ

Contents

Contents

PRAYER

"Om Bhadram Karnebbhih Shrunuyaama DevaahBhadram Pashyemaakshabhiryajatraah SthiraiangaistushtuvaamsastanoobhihVyashema Devahitam YadaayuhSwasti Na Indro VridhashravaahSwasti Nah Pooshaa VishwavedaahSwasti Nastaarkshyo ArishtanemihSwasti No Brihaspatir DadhaatuOm Shantih, Shantih, Shantih"

The literal meaning of this mantra is: OM. O Gods! Let us hear auspicious words from our ears. O reverent Gods! Let us behold propitious visions from our eyes, let our organs and body be stable, healthy, and strong. Let us do that which is pleasing to the gods in the life span allotted to us. May Indra, inscribed in the scriptures, bring us fortune! May Pushan, the knower of the world, grant us prosperity! May Trakshya, who vanquishes enemies, bestow us with blessings! May Brihaspati bring us success!
OM Peace, Peace, Peace.

About The Author

Dr. Jagadeesh Pillai is a renowned Guinness World Record holder, writer, and researcher hailing from Varanasi, also known as the abode of Lord Shiva. With a Ph.D. in Vedic Science and a range of creative ideas and achievements, he is a true polymath. He is the author of more than 100 books including Research Publications. Although his roots can be traced back to Kerala, the people of Varanasi hold him in high regard and affectionately consider him one of their own.

In 1998, Dr. Pillai was offered a job at Banaras Hindu University, but he left the position after only two months to pursue greater goals in life. He believed that in order to study Indian scriptures and engage in other creative endeavours, he needed to retire from the daily grind of working solely for money at a young age.

He started an export business from scratch, using the knowledge he had gained from a previous job in the industry. His intelligence and unique approach to business led to great success in a short period of time, earning him more in just a decade and a half than he would have in a lifetime working in a government job. Upon the passing of Dr. APJ Abdul Kalam, Dr. Pillai decided to leave the business and dedicate himself to reading, studying, researching, and experimenting.

During his tenure in the export business, Dr. Pillai traveled to over 16 countries, gaining valuable insight and experiencing the world and life in detail.

Dr. Pillai has achieved four Guinness World Records in the following subjects:

"Script to Screen" - In this record, Dr. Pillai produced and directed an animation film within the shortest time possible, breaking the previous record set by Canadians. He has also received numerous national and international awards and recognitions for this achievement.

Longest Line of Postcards - For this record, Dr. Pillai created a line of 16,300 postcards on the occasion of the 163rd anniversary of Indian Postal Day. The event also included a questionnaire about the Indian flag.

Largest Poster Awareness Campaign - Dr. Pillai designed an awareness campaign on the subject of "Beti Bachao - Beti Padhao" (Save the Girl Child - Educate the Girl Child) to achieve this record.

Largest Envelope - In tribute to the Indian Prime Minister's "Make in India" initiative, Dr. Pillai created a 4000 square meter envelope using waste paper to achieve this record.

Attempted - **70000 Candles on a 210 kg Cake** - To celebrate the 70th Indian Independence Day, Dr. Pillai attempted to light 70,000 candles on a 210 kg cake, which was recorded in World Records India.

Attempted - **Documentary on Dhamek Stupa of Sarnath in 17 Languages** - Dr. Pillai attempted to create a documentary on the Dhamek Stupa of Sarnath, dubbing it in 17 different languages. The result of this attempt is currently awaiting confirmation from the Guinness World Records.

Dr. Pillai is skilled in teaching the Bhagavad Gita, a Hindu scripture, and is popular among young people. He has helped many young people improve their lives through his motivational teachings.

In addition to teaching, he has composed and sung numerous Sanskrit Bhajans and patriotic songs.

He has also written and directed several short films and documentaries for awareness campaigns, and has volunteered with the police in both UP and Kerala to spread awareness about various issues through videos and photography.

Incredibly, he has produced and directed over 100 documentaries about the city of Varanasi, all on his own.

He has also helped and guided more than 25 boys and girls to achieve world records through creative and innovative methods. He is a multifaceted person who uses his intellect and the blessings given to him by God to excel in various areas. He is both a teacher and a student, always learning and teaching, and is able to master any subject he comes across.

He is a selfless social activist and motivational speaker who has overcome struggles and failures to become a successful and enthusiastic individual with a rich life experience.

In addition to his work with the Bhagavad Gita, he is also an efficient Tarot card reader, Astro-Vastu consultant, and a talented singer and composer. He has sung the entire Ram Charita Manas and Bhagavad Gita in his own compositions, and has sung the phrase "Lokah Samastha Sukhino Bhavantu" in 50 different languages. He is currently working on a detailed and scientific study of Vedas, Upanishads, Puranas, and the Bhagavad Gita. He has also composed and sung the Hanuman Chalisa and Gayatri Mantra in 108 and 1008 different compositions, respectively.

Awards - Four Times Guinness World Records, Winner of Mahatma Gandhi Vishwa Shanti Puraskar, Mahatma Gandhi Global Peace Ambassador, Kashi Ratna Award, Dr. APJ Abdul Kalam Motivational Person of the Year 2017, Mother Teresa Award, Indira Gandhi Priyadarshini Award, Bharat Vikas Ratna Award, Udyog Ratna Award, Vigyan Prasar Award, Poorvanchal Ratn Samman.

PREFACE

In this book, "Affirming Your Self-Worth: Strategies for Achieving Emotional Wellbeing," we will explore the importance of self-worth and how it impacts our emotional wellbeing. Self-worth is the belief in one's own value and abilities, and it is essential for leading a fulfilling and happy life.

This book is for anyone who has ever struggled with feelings of inadequacy or low self-esteem, or for those who want to build their self-worth to achieve emotional wellbeing. It is for those who want to learn strategies for affirming their self-worth and improving their emotional wellbeing.

We will cover a wide range of topics including recognizing and challenging negative self-talk, building self-esteem through positive affirmations, setting boundaries and learning to say "no", overcoming fear of failure and rejection, managing emotions, understanding and managing self-criticism, developing a growth mindset, building resilience and coping with setbacks, building a support system, connecting with others, finding and pursuing your passions, understanding and managing perfectionism, building self-compassion, the power of gratitude, and mindfulness.

This book will provide you with the tools you need to build your self-worth, improve your emotional wellbeing, and lead a fulfilling life. It is my hope that by reading this book, you will gain the understanding, knowledge, and confidence to take control of your emotional wellbeing and affirm your self-worth.

I

Understanding Self-Worth and Its Impact on Emotional Well-Being

In this chapter, we will explore the concept of self-worth and its impact on emotional wellbeing. We will discuss how self-worth is formed, how it affects our emotional wellbeing, and how we can use strategies to affirm our self-worth and improve our emotional wellbeing.

Self-worth is the value we place on ourselves and our sense of self-esteem. It is formed through our experiences, relationships, and environment. It is the foundation of our emotional wellbeing and can have a profound impact on our mental health. When we have a healthy sense of self-worth, we are more likely to have positive relationships, be resilient in the face of adversity, and have a greater sense of purpose and meaning in our lives.

On the other hand, when our self-worth is low, we are more likely to experience negative emotions such as depression, anxiety, and low self-esteem. We may also be more likely to engage in unhealthy behaviors such as substance abuse, self-harm, and other forms of self-destructive behavior.

Fortunately, there are strategies we can use to affirm our self-worth and improve our emotional wellbeing. These strategies include developing a positive self-image, setting realistic goals, engaging in positive self-talk, and engaging in activities that bring us joy. We can also practice self-care, such as getting enough sleep, eating a balanced diet, and exercising regularly.

By understanding self-worth and its impact on emotional wellbeing, we can take steps to affirm our self-worth and improve our emotional wellbeing. In this chapter, we will explore the concept of self-worth and its impact on emotional wellbeing, discuss how it is formed, and provide strategies for affirming our self-worth and improving our emotional wellbeing. By the end of this chapter, readers will have a better understanding of the importance of positive self-talk and its role in enhancing their self-esteem and overall mental health.

"Self-worth is not something that can be given to you; it must be earned through your own actions and beliefs."

ཌ ད

II

Recognizing and Challenging Negative Self-Talk

Negative self-talk can be defined as any internal dialogue that is critical, judgmental, or pessimistic. It can manifest in many forms, such as self-doubt, self-criticism, and feelings of inadequacy. It can also be expressed through negative thoughts about our physical appearance, our abilities, or our worth.

The first step in recognizing and challenging negative self-talk is to become aware of it. Pay attention to the thoughts that come into your mind and the words you use to describe yourself. Notice if you are being overly critical or judgmental. Once you become aware of your negative self-talk, you can start to challenge it.

One way to challenge negative self-talk is to ask yourself if the thought is true. Is it really true that you are not good enough? Is it really true that you are not worthy? Chances are, the answer is no.

Another way to challenge negative self-talk is to replace it with positive affirmations. Instead of telling yourself that you are not good enough, tell yourself that you are capable and worthy. Instead of telling yourself that you are not attractive, tell yourself that you are beautiful.

Finally, it is important to practice self-compassion. Instead of beating yourself up for having negative thoughts, be kind and understanding. Remind yourself that everyone has negative thoughts from time to time, and that it is okay.

Recognizing and challenging negative self-talk is an important step in achieving emotional wellbeing. By becoming aware of our inner dialogue, challenging our negative thoughts, and practicing self-compassion, we can start to create a more positive and affirming inner narrative.

"Your self-worth is determined by how you view yourself, not by how others view you."

ꙮ

III

Building Self-Esteem through Positive Affirmations

Positive affirmations are a great tool for building self-esteem, as they can help to reprogram the mind and create a more positive outlook.

In this chapter, we will explore the power of positive affirmations and how they can be used to build self-esteem. We will discuss the importance of self-esteem and how it affects our overall wellbeing. We will also look at how to create positive affirmations and how to use them to create a more positive mindset. Finally, we will discuss the importance of self-care and how it can help to further enhance self-esteem.

Positive affirmations are powerful tools for building self-esteem. They can help to reprogram the mind and create a more positive outlook. By repeating positive affirmations, we can begin to believe in ourselves and our abilities. This can help to increase our self-confidence and self-esteem.

Self-esteem is an important part of our overall wellbeing. It affects our relationships, our career, and our overall happiness. When we have a healthy self-esteem, we are more likely to take risks, be more confident, and have a more positive outlook on life.

Creating positive affirmations is an important part of building self-esteem. It is important to choose affirmations that are meaningful and that resonate with us. We can also use affirmations to help us focus on our goals and to remind us of our worth.

Using positive affirmations is only one part of building self-esteem. It is also important to practice self-care. Self-care can include activities such as exercise, meditation, and spending time with friends and family. These activities can help to reduce stress, increase feelings of happiness and contentment, and foster a sense of self-worth and acceptance. Additionally, setting and achieving personal goals, learning new skills, and engaging in creative or hobby pursuits can also contribute to building self-esteem and improving emotional wellbeing. It's important to find what works for you and make self-care a regular part of your routine.

"The key to emotional wellbeing is to recognize and accept your own worth."

ꙮ

IV

Setting Boundaries and Learning to Say "No"

Learning to set boundaries and say no is an essential part of affirming your self-worth and achieving emotional wellbeing. It can be difficult to do, however, as it requires us to be honest with ourselves and others about our needs and limits. This chapter will explore the importance of setting boundaries and saying no, and provide strategies for doing so in a way that is respectful and empowering.

Boundaries are essential for protecting our emotional wellbeing. They help us to define our limits and communicate our needs to others. When we set boundaries, we are saying no to behaviors or requests that are not in line with our values or that would cause us harm. Saying no can be difficult, but it is an important part of taking care of ourselves and asserting our autonomy.

When setting boundaries, it is important to be clear and direct. We should be honest about our needs and limits, and communicate them in a respectful way. It is also important to be mindful of our body language and tone of voice, as these can convey our message more effectively than words alone.

Learning to say no is also an important part of setting boundaries. Saying no can be difficult, as it requires us to be assertive and stand up for ourselves. It is important to remember that saying no does not make us selfish or unkind; rather, it is a way of taking care of ourselves and protecting our emotional wellbeing.

When saying no, it is important to be direct and honest. We should be clear about our needs and limits, and communicate them in a respectful way. We should also be mindful of our body language and tone of voice, as these can convey our message more effectively than words alone.

Setting boundaries and learning to say no are essential skills for affirming our self-worth and achieving emotional wellbeing. By being honest about our needs and limits, and communicating them in a respectful way, we can protect our emotional wellbeing and assert our autonomy. With practice, we can become more confident in setting boundaries and become better equipped to handle challenging situations without sacrificing our well-being. Setting boundaries can also help to reduce stress and increase our sense of control in life, leading to greater peace of mind and emotional stability. It's important to remember that setting boundaries is not about being selfish or unkind to others, but rather about taking care of ourselves and making sure we have the emotional resources to meet our own needs and the needs of others.

"Your self-worth is not dependent on the opinions of others; it is determined by your own beliefs and values."

ꕥ

V

Overcoming Fear of Failure and Rejection

The first step in overcoming fear of failure and rejection is to recognize that these feelings are normal. Everyone experiences fear of failure and rejection at some point in their lives. It is important to acknowledge these feelings and understand that they are a natural part of life. Once you have accepted that these feelings are normal, you can begin to take steps to address them.

The next step is to identify the source of your fear. Is it a fear of not being good enough? A fear of not being accepted? A fear of not being able to achieve your goals? Once you have identified the source of your fear, you can begin to take steps to address it.

One way to address fear of failure and rejection is to focus on the positive. Instead of focusing on the potential for failure, focus on the potential for success. Remind yourself of your strengths and accomplishments, and focus on the things that you can do to increase your chances of success.

Another way to address fear of failure and rejection is to practice self-compassion. Instead of beating yourself up for not being perfect, be kind to yourself. Remind yourself that everyone makes mistakes and that it is okay to make mistakes.

Finally, it is important to take action. Instead of letting fear of failure and rejection paralyze you, take action. Set goals and take steps to achieve them. This will help you to build confidence and reduce your fear of failure and rejection.

By recognizing that fear of failure and rejection is normal, identifying the source of your fear, focusing on the positive, practicing self-compassion, and seeking support from friends and loved ones, we can overcome fear and build resilience. Facing our fears can help us to gain confidence and overcome obstacles, leading to personal growth and improved self-esteem. It's also important to remember that failure is a natural part of life, and that it is often from our failures that we learn and grow the most. Instead of focusing on the negative aspects of failure, it can be helpful to focus on what we can learn from the experience and how we can apply this knowledge to future opportunities. With the right mindset and support, we can develop the courage to take risks, pursue our dreams, and lead a fulfilling life.

"The most important step in affirming your self-worth is to recognize and appreciate your own unique strengths and abilities."

☙

VI

Managing Emotions: The Importance of Self-Care

Self-care is a way to show respect for oneself and to ensure that one's emotional wellbeing is maintained.

When it comes to managing emotions, self-care is key. It is important to take time to relax, reflect, and practice self-care activities such as yoga, meditation, journaling, and spending time in nature. These activities can help to reduce stress and anxiety, and can help to create a sense of balance and inner peace. Additionally, self-care can help to foster a sense of self-worth and self-confidence.

Self-care is also important for managing difficult emotions. It is important to recognize that emotions are a normal part of life, and that it is okay to feel them. Taking time to practice self-care activities can help to process and manage difficult emotions in a healthy way. Additionally, self-care can help to create a sense of safety and security, which can be especially helpful when dealing with difficult emotions.

Finally, self-care is important for affirming one's self-worth. Taking time to practice self-care activities can help to create a sense of self-love and self-acceptance. Additionally, self-care can help to foster a sense of self-confidence and self-esteem. By taking time to practice self-care, one can learn to appreciate and value themselves, which is essential for affirming one's self-worth.

In conclusion, self-care is an essential part of managing emotions and affirming one's self-worth. Taking time to practice self-care activities can help to reduce stress and anxiety, process and manage difficult emotions in a healthy way, and foster a sense of self-love and self-acceptance. Self-care also involves setting boundaries and learning to say no, as well as developing coping mechanisms for handling fear and failure. By prioritizing self-care, building self-esteem, and adopting a positive outlook, we can improve our emotional wellbeing and lead a more fulfilling life. Remember, self-care is a journey, and it's important to be patient and kind to ourselves as we work towards our goals.

"Self-worth is not something that can be achieved overnight; it is a journey of self-discovery and growth."

ꟸ

VII

Understanding and Managing Self-Criticism

Self-criticism is a common issue that many people struggle with. It can be a source of immense stress and can lead to feelings of low self-worth. To effectively manage self-criticism, it is important to understand the underlying causes and develop strategies to address them.

First, it is important to recognize that self-criticism is often rooted in a fear of failure. People may be afraid to take risks or try new things because they are afraid of being judged or criticized by others. This fear can lead to a cycle of self-criticism and low self-esteem.

Second, it is important to recognize that self-criticism is often a result of negative self-talk. People may be engaging in negative self-talk without even realizing it. This can lead to feelings of inadequacy and low self-esteem.

Third, it is important to recognize that self-criticism can be a result of perfectionism. People may be striving for perfection in all aspects of their lives, which can lead to feelings of frustration and disappointment.

Finally, it is important to recognize that self-criticism can be a result of comparing oneself to others. People may be comparing themselves to others in terms of success, appearance, or other areas, which can lead to feelings of inadequacy and low self-esteem.

Once the underlying causes of self-criticism have been identified, it is important to develop strategies to address them. This can include engaging in positive self-talk, setting realistic goals, and focusing on one's strengths and accomplishments.

Additionally, it is important to practice self-compassion and to recognize that mistakes are part of the learning process. Rather than punishing oneself for perceived shortcomings, it can be helpful to focus on growth and improvement. Challenging negative self-talk and replacing it with positive affirmations can also help to shift the mindset towards self-acceptance and compassion.

Finally, seeking support from friends, loved ones, or a therapist can provide valuable perspective, encouragement, and tools for addressing self-criticism and building self-esteem. Remember, it takes time and effort to change negative self-talk patterns, but with dedication and support, it is possible to overcome self-criticism and lead a life filled with self-love and happiness.

"The best way to affirm your self-worth is to focus on your positive qualities and accomplishments."

ꟹ

VIII

Developing a Growth Mindset

Developing a growth mindset is essential for achieving emotional wellbeing. A growth mindset is the belief that one's abilities and intelligence can be developed and improved over time. It is the opposite of a fixed mindset, which is the belief that one's abilities and intelligence are fixed and cannot be changed.

Having a growth mindset can help us to become more resilient in the face of adversity and to take risks that can lead to personal growth. It can also help us to develop a greater sense of self-worth and to become more confident in our abilities.

In order to develop a growth mindset, it is important to focus on the process of learning and growth rather than the outcome. We should strive to learn from our mistakes and to take risks that can lead to personal growth. We should also focus on our strengths and use them to our advantage.

It is also important to be mindful of our thoughts and to challenge any negative thoughts that may be holding us back. We should strive to replace negative thoughts with positive ones and to focus on our successes rather than our failures.

Finally, it is important to practice self-compassion. We should strive to be kind to ourselves and to recognize that we are all human and make mistakes. We should also strive to be patient with ourselves and to recognize that growth takes time.

By developing a growth mindset, we can become more resilient in the face of adversity, take risks that can lead to personal growth, and develop a greater sense of self-worth. We can also become more mindful of our thoughts and practice self-compassion. By doing so, we can take steps towards achieving emotional wellbeing.

"Your self-worth is not defined by your successes or failures; it is determined by how you view yourself."

ꕤ

IX

Building Resilience and Coping with Setbacks

Resilience is the ability to bounce back from adversity and setbacks. It is a key factor in achieving emotional wellbeing, as it allows us to cope with difficult situations and move forward. Building resilience requires us to recognize our strengths and weaknesses, and to develop strategies to cope with difficult situations.

One way to build resilience is to practice self-care. This includes taking time for yourself, engaging in activities that bring you joy, and setting boundaries with others. Self-care can help you to manage stress and build emotional strength.

Another way to build resilience is to practice positive self-talk. This involves recognizing and challenging negative thoughts and replacing them with positive ones. Positive self-talk can help to boost your self-esteem and give you the confidence to face difficult situations.

Finally, it is important to practice self-compassion. This involves being kind and understanding to yourself, even when you make mistakes. Self-compassion can help to reduce feelings of guilt and shame, and can help you to move forward from setbacks.

By building resilience and coping with setbacks, you can affirm your self-worth and achieve emotional wellbeing. Through self-care, positive self-talk, and self-compassion, you can develop the skills and strategies needed to face difficult situations and move forward. With these tools, you can create a life of emotional wellbeing and self-worth.

"The most powerful way to affirm your self-worth is to practice self-compassion and self-care."

&

X

Building a Support System and Connecting with Others

Having a strong support system is essential for emotional wellbeing. It can provide a sense of security, comfort, and understanding. To build a support system, start by identifying the people in your life who you can rely on for emotional support. This could include family members, friends, colleagues, or even a therapist. Once you have identified these people, make sure to reach out to them regularly and let them know that you value their support.

In addition to having a strong support system, connecting with others is also important for emotional wellbeing. This could include joining a support group, attending social events, or even just having a conversation with a stranger.

Connecting with others can help you feel less isolated and more connected to the world around you.

Finally, it is important to remember that your self-worth is not determined by the opinions of others. Instead, it is determined by your own values and beliefs. To affirm your self-worth, focus on the things that make you unique and special. Celebrate your successes and be kind to yourself when you make mistakes.

By building a strong support system, connecting with others, and affirming your self-worth, you can achieve emotional wellbeing. With the right approach, you can create a life that is full of joy, peace, and fulfillment.

"Your self-worth is not determined by your material possessions or external achievements; it is determined by your inner strength and resilience."

ꕥ

XI

Finding and Pursuing Your Passions

The first step in finding and pursuing your passions is to identify what you are passionate about. This can be anything from a hobby or activity to a career or cause. Take some time to reflect on what you enjoy doing and what brings you joy. Consider what you are naturally drawn to and what you would like to learn more about. Once you have identified your passions, it is time to pursue them.

Start by setting realistic goals for yourself. Break down your goals into smaller, achievable steps. This will help you stay motivated and on track. Additionally, make sure to set aside time each day to work on your passions. This could be as little as 15 minutes or as much as an hour.

It is also important to find a supportive community. This

could be a group of friends or family members who share your interests or a professional organization related to your field. Having a supportive network of people who understand and encourage your passions can be invaluable.

Finally, don't be afraid to take risks. Pursuing your passions can be intimidating, but it is also incredibly rewarding. Don't be afraid to try something new or take a chance. You never know what you might discover.

Finding and pursuing your passions can be a powerful way to affirm your self-worth and achieve emotional wellbeing. By taking the time to identify what you are passionate about, setting realistic goals, finding a supportive community, and taking risks, you can unlock a world of possibilities.

"The most effective way to affirm your self-worth is to surround yourself with positive people who support and encourage you."

༄

XII

Understanding and Managing Perfectionism

Perfectionism can be a double-edged sword. On one hand, it can drive us to achieve great things, but on the other, it can be a source of immense stress and anxiety. In order to achieve emotional wellbeing, it is important to understand and manage perfectionism.

Perfectionism is often rooted in a desire to be accepted and to feel worthy. It can manifest in a variety of ways, from striving for excellence in all areas of life to setting unrealistic expectations for oneself. Perfectionism can also lead to procrastination, as the fear of failure can be paralyzing.

The key to managing perfectionism is to recognize it and to be mindful of its effects. It is important to be aware of the underlying motivations for perfectionism and to challenge any negative thoughts or beliefs that may be driving it. It is also important to set realistic goals and to practice self-compassion.

It is also important to recognize that perfectionism is not always a bad thing. It can be a source of motivation and can help us to strive for excellence. However, it is important to be mindful of the potential pitfalls of perfectionism and to practice self-care.

Finally, it is important to remember that perfectionism is not a measure of self-worth. It is important to recognize that mistakes are part of the learning process and to focus on the progress that has been made, rather than on the mistakes that have been made.

By understanding and managing perfectionism, we can achieve emotional wellbeing. By recognizing the underlying motivations for perfectionism, setting realistic goals, and practicing self-compassion and self-care, we can learn to embrace our imperfections and to focus on our progress. By doing so, we can learn to affirm our self-worth and to achieve emotional wellbeing.

"Your self-worth is not determined by your past; it is determined by your present and future actions."

☙

XIII

Affirmations to Achieve Emotional Wellbeing

Positive affirmations are powerful tools for achieving emotional wellbeing. They can help to shift our mindset and create a more positive outlook on life. This chapter will provide a list of positive affirmations that can be used to help promote emotional wellbeing.

Positive affirmations can be used to help us focus on the positive aspects of our lives and to create a more positive outlook. They can also help to reduce stress and anxiety, and to increase our self-confidence and self-esteem.

The following is a list of positive affirmations that can be used to help promote emotional wellbeing:

1. I am worthy of love and respect.

2. I am capable of achieving my goals.

3. I am strong and resilient.

4. I am worthy of success.

5. I am capable of making positive changes in my life.

6. I am worthy of happiness and joy.

7. I am capable of overcoming any obstacle.

8. I am worthy of living a life of abundance.

9. I am capable of creating a life of purpose and meaning.

10. I am worthy of living a life of fulfillment.

By repeating these affirmations on a daily basis, we can begin to create a more positive outlook on life and to achieve emotional wellbeing. Positive affirmations can help to reduce stress and anxiety, and to increase our self-confidence and self-esteem. They can also help to create a more positive mindset and to create a life of purpose and meaning.

Positive affirmations are powerful tools for achieving emotional wellbeing. By repeating these affirmations on a daily basis, we can begin to create a more positive outlook on life and to achieve emotional wellbeing. With consistent practice, these affirmations can help to reduce stress and anxiety, and to increase our self-confidence and self-esteem.

They can also help to change negative thought patterns and foster a sense of self-love and self-acceptance. It's important to choose affirmations that resonate with you and to repeat them regularly, whether it be in the morning, before bed, or throughout the day.

Additionally, pairing affirmations with visualization techniques and positive self-talk can enhance their effectiveness. However, it's important to remember that affirmations alone are not a cure for mental health concerns, and it may be helpful to seek support from a mental health professional if you are experiencing significant emotional distress.

With patience and persistence, positive affirmations can be a powerful tool in promoting emotional wellbeing and personal growth.

"The best way to affirm your self-worth is to focus on your personal growth and development."

ꕤ

XIV
Building Self-Compassion

Self-compassion is the practice of being kind and understanding to oneself, even in the face of difficult emotions or challenging situations. It is an essential part of emotional wellbeing, as it helps us to accept ourselves and our experiences, rather than judging or criticizing ourselves.

The first step in building self-compassion is to recognize that we are all imperfect and that it is okay to make mistakes. We can start by acknowledging our own humanity and recognizing that we are not alone in our struggles. We can also practice self-forgiveness, allowing ourselves to move on from our mistakes and learn from them.

Next, we can practice self-kindness. This involves treating ourselves with the same kindness and understanding that we would show to a friend or loved one. We can do this by speaking to ourselves in a gentle and understanding way, and by engaging in activities that bring us joy and relaxation.

Finally, we can practice mindfulness. This involves being present in the moment and observing our thoughts and feelings without judgment. Mindfulness can help us to recognize our emotions and accept them without trying to change them.

By practicing these three steps, we can begin to build self-compassion and cultivate emotional wellbeing. With time and practice, we can learn to accept ourselves and our experiences, and to be kind and understanding to ourselves. This can help us to feel more connected to ourselves and to the world around us, and to live a more fulfilling and meaningful life.

"Your self-worth is not determined by your mistakes; it is determined by how you learn and grow from them."

ꕤ

XV

The power of Gratitude and Mindfulness

Gratitude and mindfulness are powerful tools for achieving emotional wellbeing. In this chapter of "Affirming Your Self-Worth Strategies for Achieving Emotional Wellbeing," we will explore how these two practices can help you cultivate a sense of self-worth and emotional balance.

Gratitude is the practice of recognizing and appreciating the good in our lives. It can be as simple as taking a few moments each day to reflect on the things we are thankful for. This can be anything from the beauty of nature to the kindness of a friend. By taking the time to recognize and appreciate the good in our lives, we can cultivate a sense of contentment and joy.

Mindfulness is the practice of being present in the moment.

It involves being aware of our thoughts, feelings, and sensations without judgment. By being mindful, we can become more aware of our emotions and how they affect our behavior. This can help us to better understand our needs and make decisions that are in line with our values.

When we combine gratitude and mindfulness, we can create a powerful tool for achieving emotional wellbeing. By taking the time to recognize and appreciate the good in our lives, we can cultivate a sense of contentment and joy. By being mindful of our thoughts, feelings, and sensations, we can become more aware of our emotions and how they affect our behavior. This can help us to better understand our needs and make decisions that are in line with our values.

Gratitude and mindfulness can be powerful tools for achieving emotional wellbeing. By taking the time to recognize and appreciate the good in our lives, and by being mindful of our thoughts, feelings, and sensations, we can cultivate a sense of self-worth and emotional balance. With regular practice, we can learn to use these tools to create a life of joy, contentment, and emotional wellbeing.

The most important thing to remember when affirming your self-worth is to be kind and gentle to yourself."

ꟸ

Other Books Of The Author

1. The Moments When I Met God
2. Kashiyile Theertha Pathangal
3. GURU GYAN VANI
4. Abhiprerak Gita
5. ASSI SE JAIN GHAT TAK
6. Hopelessness of Arjuna
7. The Soul and It's True Nature
8. Sense of Action (Karma)
9. Action through Wisdom
10. Action through Wisdom
11. THEORY AND PRACTICAL OF EVERY ACTION
12. LOGICAL UNDERSTANDING OF THE SUPREME
13. THE IMPERISHABLE SUPREME
14. Yatra Nishadraj se Hanuman Ghat Tak
15. Yatra Karnatak Ghat se Raja Ghat Tak
16. Yatra Pandey Ghat se Prayagraj Ghat Tak
17. Yatra Ranjendra Prasad Ghat se Dattatreya Ghat Tak
18. YaatraSindhiya Ghat se Gwaliar Ghat Tak
19. Yatra Mangala Gauri Ghat se Hanuman Gadhi Ghat Tak
20. Yatra Gaay Ghat Se Nishad Ghat Tak
21. MAA GANGA, GHATEN EVM UTSAV
22. Ganga Arti Dev Deepavali evam Any Utsav
23. Potentials of Digitalized India
24. VEDIC CONSCIOUSNESS
25. A Brief Introduction to Vedic Science
26. Kashi ke Barah Jyotirling
27. IMPACT OF MOTIVATION
28. Let's have a Milky Way Journey
29. Color Therapy in a Nutshell

30. Rigveda in a Nutshell
31. Yajurveda in a Nutshell
32. Samveda in a Nutshell
33. Atharva Veda in a Nutshell
34. Ayushman Bhava - Ayurveda
35. Srimad Bhagavad Gita and Upanishad Connection
36. Srimad Bhagavad Gita - an attempt to summarize each chapter.
37. Facts and Impact of Nakshatra
38. Astro Gems - NAVARATNA
39. Ekadashi - A Concise Overview
40. A Concise View of Hanuman Chalisa
41. Inspirational Gita
42. Nakshatraranyam
43. Summary of 18 Mahapuranas
44. Synopsis of 18 Upa Puranas
45. Rigvediya Upanishads
46. Shukla Yajurvediya Upanishads
47. Krishna Yajurvediya Upanishads
48. Samavediya Upanishads
49. Atharvavediya Upanishads
50. The Seven Great Sages
51. From Rocket Scientist to President Dr. APJ Abdul Kalam
52. The Visionary's Voice - Quotes of Dr. APJ Abdul Kalam
53. The Wisdom of Swami Vivekananda: Insights and Inspiration from a Legendary Spiritual Teacher
54. Ayurvedic Remedies from the Garden
55. Sages and Seers
56. Rising Strong – Motivational Stories of Women
57. Beyond Flames -Mystery stories of Funeral Ghat Manikarnika
58. The Origins of Tulsi: A Look at the Mythological Roots of the Plant"

59. The Holistic Cow: A Look at the Physical, Spiritual, and Cultural Importance of Cows in India
60. Arts of Healing
61. Exploring the Divine
62. Understanding Five Elements
63. The Etymology of Ram
64. Symbols of India
65. Voice of Change (About Speeches of Great Men)
66. She Speaks (About Speeches of Great Women)
67. Patriotism on Celluloid – Brief About Patriotic Films
68. The Music of Motivation: A Brief Guide to Inspirational Film Songs
69. **Unlocking the Secrets of the Dashopanishads**
70. A Cultural Mosaic
71. Ancient Traditions, Modern Minds
72. Ecos of Ancient Wisdom
73. Beneath the Surface
74. From Temples to Ashrams
75. Sages of the Subcontinent
76. The Art of Healling (Ayurveda, Yoga & Naturopathy)
77. Indian Kitchen
78. The Festivals of India
79. The Indian Epics Retold
80. The Power of Mantras
81. The Indian River Ganges
82. The Indian Architecture
83. Rites of Passage
84. The Indian Silk Road
85. The Indian Literature
86. The Indian Villages
87. The Indian Folks & Crafts
88. The Way of Buddha
89. The Ramayan of Tulsidas

90. Astrological Remedies
91. The Secret Power of Motivation
92. Secret of Developing your Inner Strength
93. The Secret Path to Motivation
94. The Art and Secret of Positive Thinking
95. The Secrets of Practicing Ethical Living
96. Indian Art and Painting
97. The Indian Herbalism
98. Bharatanatyam to Kathak
99. Exploring India's Astrological Remedies
100. The Indian Festival of Flowers
101. Indian Handicrafts
102. The Splashes of Joy – India's Colour Festival
103. The Indian Science of Astrology
104. The Indian Mythology
105. Path to Enlightenment
106. The Indian Spirituality for Children
107. Aromas of India
108. The Secrets of Healthy Relationships
109. Ancestral Ties
110. The Indian Street Food
111. Discovering America
112. The Indian Textile
113. Listening to Motivational Speeches
114. Taste of India
115. A Cultural Journey through Indian Nuptials
116. Motivational Quote for Change
117. Secret Strategies for Making Money
118. Secrets to Cultivate a Positive Mindset
119. A Tapestry of Cultures: Exploring India from Kashmir to Kanyakumari
120. Achieving Your Dreams with Resilience: Secret Strategies for Overcoming Obstacles

121. Innovative Startups - 25 Startup Ideas to Spark Your Business Creativity
122. Export Management: Strategies for Global Success
123. Exporting from India - A Step by Step Guide
124. Finance Fundamentals: Mastering Financial Management for Business Success
125. Global Growth Strategies for International Business Development
126. Marketing Mastery: Unlocking the Secrets of Modern Marketing
127. Operations Mastery: Managing the Flow of Value in Business
128. Strategic Business Management: Navigating the Modern Business Landscape
129. Human Resource Management Strategies for Building and Managing a High Performance Team
130. The Indian Landscapes and Nature: An Exploration Of India's Natural Beauty And Diversity
131. The Indian Street Performances: A Cultural Exploration of India's Street Performances
132. Affirming Your Self-Worth: Strategies for Achieving Emotional Wellbeing
133. Cultivating Self-Discipline: Secrets Methods for Achieving Your Goals
134. Embracing Change: Strategies for Adapting to Life's Challenges
135. Embracing Your Uniqueness: Secret Strategies for Living an Authentic Life
136. Finding Motivation in Despondency: Coping with Difficult Times

Contact

DR. JAGADEESH PILLAI

MBA & PhD in Vedic Science

Four Times Guinness World Record Holder

Winner of Mahatma Gandhi Vishwa Shanti Puraskar and Global Peace Ambassador

Gemology, Astro & Vastu Consultant - Spiritual Counselor

Consultant for designing World Record Ideas

Efficient Tarot Card Reader

9839093003

myrichindia@gmail.com

drjagadeeshpillai@facebook

drjagadeeshpillai@instagram

jagadeeshpillai@youtube

www. JAGADEESHPILLAI.com

|| LOKAHA SAMASTHAHA SUKHINO BHAVANTU ||

Printed by Libri Plureos GmbH in Hamburg,
Germany

9 798889 592358